Would You Rather Game Book For Kids and Family

200 Funny Scenarios, Wacky Choices and Hilarious Situations for the Whole Family

With Fun Illustrations

Riddleland

Table of Contents

Introduction

"It is not the answer that enlightens, but the question" – Eugene Jonesco

We would like to personally thank you for purchasing this book. **Would you rather game book for kids and family** is a collection of 200 of the funniest scenarios, wacky choices, and hilarious situations for the family to choose from. It is also filled with fun and cute illustrations.

These questions are an excellent way to get a conversation started in a fun and exciting way. Also, by asking "Why" after a "would you rather question", you may find interesting answers and learn a lot about a person.

We wrote this book because we want children to be encouraged to read more, think and grow. As parents, we know that when children play games and learn, they are being educated whilst having so much fun that they don't even realize they're learning and developing valuable life skills. 'Would you Rather …' is one of our favorite games to play as a family. Some of the 'would you rather …' scenarios have had us in fits of giggles, others have generated reactions such as: "eeeeeeuuugh that's gross!" and yet others still really make us think and reflect and consider our decisions.

Beside have fun, playing the game also has other benefits such as:

- **Communication** – This game helps children to interact, read aloud and listen to others. It's a great way to connect. It's a fun way for parents to get their children interacting with them, without a formal awkward conversation. The game can help to get to know someone better and learn about their likes, dislikes, and values.

- **Builds Confidence** – Children get used to pronouncing vocabulary, asking questions and it helps to deal with shyness.

- **Develops Critical Thinking** – It helps children to defend and justify the rationale for their choices and can generate discussions and debates. Parents playing this game with young children can give them prompting questions about their answers to help them reach logical and sensible decisions.

- **Improves Vocabulary** – Children will be introduced to new words in the questions, and the context of them will help them remember them because the game is fun.

- **Encourages Equality and Diversity** – Considering other people's answers, even if they differ from your own, it is important for respect, equality, diversity, tolerance, acceptance, and inclusivity. Some questions may get children to think about options available to them, that don't fall into gendered stereotypes, i.e., careers or activities that challenge the norm.

Rules of the Games

This game is probably best played with other people, so if you can, play it with friends or family.

If you have two players

- Player 1 takes the book and asks the player 2 a question beginning with the phrase "Would you rather...? Why?
- After player 2 made his/her choice, he/she would have to explain the reason why the choice was made.
- Pass the book to the other player, and they ask you a question.
- Learn lots about one another, have fun and giggles.
- The Two-Player game version could work well as an ice-breaker exercise prior to introductions in classes or meetings.

If you have three or four players

- Out of your group decide who will be the question master. If you can't decide, have folded bits of paper with 'Question Master' written on one, and 'players' on the other and each pick one.

- The question Master asks one question from the book.

- The other two or three people give their answers.

- The Question Master decides who has given the best answer – this is the answer with the best explanation for why. The explanations can be funny, or creative or well thought out. The Question Master's decision is final. One point is given for the best answer. If the Question Master can't decide, both players get one point each.

- The first player to reach a score of 10 points wins.

LET THE FUN BEGIN!

Alert: Riddleland Bonus

Join our exclusive Facebook Group

at

Riddleland For Kids

or

send an email to:

Riddleland@riddlelandforkids.com

and you will get the following

• 50 Bonus Jokes and Riddles

• An entry in our Monthly Giveaway of a $25

Amazon Gift card!

• Early Access to new books

We draw a new winner each month and will
contact you via email or the Facebook group.
Good Luck!

WOULD YOU RATHER....

Live in a house made of chocolate
or
gummi bears?

Have long hair down to the floor

or

a furry hairy body everywhere?

WOULD YOU RATHER...

Have a tail that wags when you meet
your friends

Or

a nose that grows when you lie?

Go on a family holiday

or

pick 5 toys of your choice for your
birthday?

WOULD YOU RATHER...

Be an eagle that can swim

or

A salmon that can walk on land

Brush your teeth with a used
toothbrush

or

go to use a toilet that has no toilet
paper?

WOULD YOU RATHER...

Eat fried strawberries
or
green beans ice cream?

Take a picture of every single meal and
post it on Facebook

or

report to your mommy every time you
ate any junk food like chocolate,
cakes, crisps, etc?

WOULD YOU RATHER...

Be a crocodile without teeth

or

a snapping turtle?

Give a loud hiccup every time someone
says your name
or
get a fit of giggles every time you say
goodbye?

WOULD YOU RATHER...

Ride on a magic carpet
or
on a rocket?

Be able to climb walls like spiderman
or
be able to turn your friends into
cartoons?

WOULD YOU RATHER...

Eat chocolate cake
or
Carrot cake for breakfast?

Eat a plate spaghetti with caramel
sauce
or

a scoop of barbeque flavored ice
cream?

WOULD YOU RATHER...

Have one large eye
or
four ears?

Have no hair

or

breath that stinks?

WOULD YOU RATHER...

Visit an ice-hotel
Or
go to a Beauty Spa?

Go to the circus show with no clowns
Or
the zoo with no animals?

WOULD YOU RATHER...

Drink water

or

milk each mealtime?

Have a go in a go-kart
or
fly a kite?

WOULD YOU RATHER...

Have dragon's wings
or
a puppy dog's tail?

Have a dragon's tail

or

a unicorn's horn?

WOULD YOU RATHER...

Have a pig's snout for a nose

or

a beaver's teeth?

Live till 100 years old

or

live forever but not able to eat anything?

WOULD YOU RATHER...

Eat raw carrots
or
fresh apples for a whole week?

Wear a thick Eskimo jacket
or
a Scottish Kilt for a whole summer?

WOULD YOU RATHER...

Have curly hair that turns pink when you straighten

Or

straight hair that turns purple when you curled it?

Never need to wash your hair

Or

never need to cut your nails?

WOULD YOU RATHER...

Make a cock-a-doodle-doo noise when you yawn,
Or
make a bleating lamb sound each time you laugh?

Lick a dirty rubbish bin

or

lick a bathroom floor?

WOULD YOU RATHER...

Be very tall

or

very small?

Always sweat honey when you run
or
always sweat chocolate when you skip
around?

WOULD YOU RATHER...

Eat a small tin of dog food

Or

eat two rotten eggs?

Go on a cruise where you visit many places for just a day,

or

spend a week on one holiday destination?

WOULD YOU RATHER...

Be scared of heights

or

have a phobia of water?

Drive an unreliable modern sportscar
that keeps breaking down
or
drive a beaten-up old banger that is
super reliable and never breaks down?

WOULD YOU RATHER...

Give up eating chocolate
or
stop eating fast food?

Walk down a busy shopping area
clucking like a chicken
or
howling like a wolf?

WOULD YOU RATHER...

Ride in a flying car
or
have a car that can land on water?

Swim through jelly
or
dive into a pool of chocolate spread?

WOULD YOU RATHER...

Be able to run faster than a leopard
Or
be stronger than an elephant?

Eat only meats
Or
only vegetables for a month?

WOULD YOU RATHER...

Have Chinese takeout noodles
or Indian curry rice for supper for 1
month?

Eat 4 Doughnuts without licking your
lips,
or
eat a lemon without puckering your
face up due to the sourness?

WOULD YOU RATHER...

Wear a blindfold
or
wear earphones when you sleep?

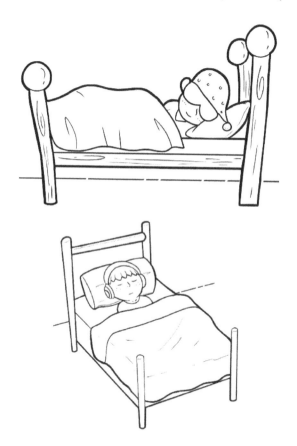

Lay in a bath tub full of worms
or
spiders?

WOULD YOU RATHER...

Live on Jupiter
Or
Uranus?

Be able to live in a submarine
Or
an airplane for 5 years?

WOULD YOU RATHER...

Eat jam doughnuts

or

custard doughnuts?

Have a job that makes a huge difference to the world, but you don't earn a lot of money

or

become famous for something fairly trivial and make a fantastic big salary because of it?

WOULD YOU RATHER...

Your toys came to life
or
that your pets could speak?

Take a bath in squirming eels,
or
crawling tarantulas?

WOULD YOU RATHER...

Have your neck as long as a giraffe

Or

your nose as long as an elephant's trunk?

Have the vision to see far away as though you're looking through a telescope,

Or

have the vision that allows you to see every minute detail like a microscope?

WOULD YOU RATHER...

Constantly speak in a whisper
or
constantly shout?

Live a long life but be poor
or
a short life but be wealthy?

WOULD YOU RATHER...

Have to walk everywhere on your hands
or
walk everywhere with your leg tied to your best friend like in a three-legged race?

Lick a dirty rubbish bin

or

lick a bathroom floor?

WOULD YOU RATHER...

Would you rather live in Mars for 1 year or

on the Moon for 1 year?

Have to roar like a lion for 2 minutes

or

scratch the waiter's head every time you are ready to order food?

WOULD YOU RATHER...

Have every item of your clothing be an identical color

or

have every item of clothing be polka dots?

Have to end every sentence with the words "with a cherry on top"

or

do cartwheels every time you have to go wash your hands?

WOULD YOU RATHER...

Turn into a hamster for a day once a month
or
turn into a parrot for one day each week?

Take a shower wearing clothes

or

wear a bathing suit to the cinema?

WOULD YOU RATHER...

Wear a huge colorful hat each day
or
shoes that are three sizes too big for you?

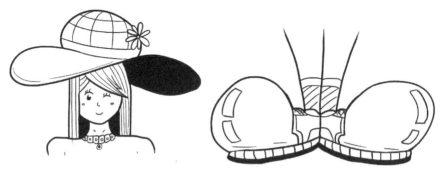

Be able to jump as high as the Empire State Building

or

be able to squeeze yourself under closed doors?

WOULD YOU RATHER...

Be active during the day like a butterfly

or

like a moth during the night?

Eat a spider
or
have 40 of them crawl over you?

WOULD YOU RATHER...

Be a knight in shining armor

or

a court jester that can fly?

Have a slide in your house from the
top floor to the ground,
or
have an underground lake with
gondolas?

WOULD YOU RATHER...

Go without dessert for a month then
be given them for two months
or
go without them for two weeks and
have them for two weeks?

Eat a scorpion
or
a grasshopper for every meal?

WOULD YOU RATHER...

Be a chef

or

a cowboy?

Blow the seeds off a dandelion
or
pick the petals off a daisy?

WOULD YOU RATHER...

Eat a plate of brussel sprouts

or

2 pieces of smoked Kippers?

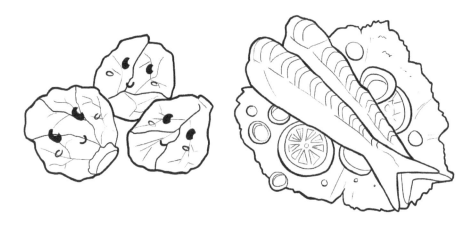

Eat your favorite food every day
or
find $3 under your pillow each
morning?

WOULD YOU RATHER...

Brush your teeth with mud,
or
wash your face with vinegar?

Have to mime everything you want to
say
or
draw everything you want to say?

WOULD YOU RATHER...

See the Great Wall of China
or
Stonehenge?

Visit the Eiffel Tower during a
thunderstorm
or
the Golden Gate Bridge during a
blizzard?

WOULD YOU RATHER...

Be a magician
or
an origami expert?

Have nails that changed color to
indicate your mood,
or
eyes that changed color depending on
how hot or cold the weather was?

WOULD YOU RATHER...

Drink a cup of vinegar
or
eat a cup of mushy peas?

Live in your own home
or
Disneyworld for your entire life?

WOULD YOU RATHER...

Have a jetpack meaning you could fly anywhere

Or

an extendable arm?

Live in a cave with 5 puppies

Or

a treehouse with 5 kittens?

WOULD YOU RATHER...

Own a life-sized robot

or

a talking car?

Have the ability to turn any carpeted
room into a swimming pool
or
fill the room with bubbles?

WOULD YOU RATHER...

Get a shot

or

stung by a bee?

Sneeze constantly for 5 minutes once a day,

or

sneeze once every 30 minutes all day?

WOULD YOU RATHER...

Meet a mermaid
or
the Loch Ness Monster?

Be given every new box of Lego that
comes out
or
every new computer game?

WOULD YOU RATHER...

Fly on the back of a dragon or on a broomstick?

Be able to jump into any painting, walk around, explore and the ability to return when you wanted
or
jump into a TV show or film and return when you wanted?

WOULD YOU RATHER...

Be unbeatable at arm-wrestling
or
toe-wrestling?

Lay in a bath full of iguanas
or
snakes?

WOULD YOU RATHER...

Change the color of your hair by pinching your nose

or

Change the color of your eyes by tightly blinking your eyes?

Wear your shoes on the wrong feet
or
your pants backward for a day?

WOULD YOU RATHER...

Drink ice-cold water for 10 years

or

warm soft drinks?

Have perfect memory for everything
you've experienced, looked at or heard
so far in life
or
be able to draw anything perfectly
from memory?

WOULD YOU RATHER...

Have a head the size of an orange

or

the size of a pumpkin?

Drink cookie dough milkshake
or
mango slushies for breakfast every
morning?

WOULD YOU RATHER...

Be as strong as a gorilla
or
as big as a whale?

Have a rare bird make a nest on your hair so that you had to carry the bird and its eggs around on top of your head until they hatched

or

that you impulsively broke out into the birdy-song and dance each time you see a bird in the street/sky?

WOULD YOU RATHER...

Lose all your teeth
or
lose all your hair?

Be only able to smell stinky things
or
never be able to smell anything ever?

WOULD YOU RATHER...

Feel constantly itchy

or

constantly tingly?

Be a cleaner for a very dirty messy
person
or
a chef for someone who eats
constantly all day?

WOULD YOU RATHER...

Drink sour milk

or

your own urine?

Stay silent for three solid hours during
the day
or
give a talk to a group of 30 students?

WOULD YOU RATHER...

Eat pizza for every meal

or

a surprise dish?

Eat the same breakfast, lunch, dinner
menu for the rest of your life,
or
only eat sweets and chocolate for the
rest of your life?

WOULD YOU RATHER...

Have ketchup with every meal
or
salt?

Be the first person on Mars

or

the President of the United States?

WOULD YOU RATHER...

Eat all your food liquified
or
raw?

Only ever be able to eat green
vegetables for the rest of your life,
or
only ever be able to eat fruits for the
rest of your life?

WOULD YOU RATHER...

Eat moldy bread
or
moldy cheese?

Never eat cheese again
or
never eat chocolate again?

WOULD YOU RATHER...

Take a bite out of a lemon
or
an onion?

That when you're out for a meal that
you can have unlimited drinks, but
only the same type of drink
or
any three different drinks of your
choosing?

WOULD YOU RATHER...

Have bacon for breakfast each day
or
a sausage for dinner each day?

Be served food by someone who has
not washed their hands
or
someone who has a cold?

WOULD YOU RATHER...

Eat a watermelon that tastes like strawberries

or

a cantaloupe melon that tastes like apples?

Have a magic freezer that has your favorite ice cream inside

or

a magic oven that produced your favorite meal each evening?

WOULD YOU RATHER...

Eat waffles
or
sausages for lunch every afternoon?

Spend a year sailing to different
countries in the world
or
spend a year living in your favorite
country abroad?

WOULD YOU RATHER...

Travel the world by hot air balloon

or

by the Orient Express?

Go to school at Hogwarts

or

find Narnia at the back of your wardrobe?

WOULD YOU RATHER...

Go camping in a tent
or
stay in a hotel?

Go air gliding
or
ride on a miniature train?

WOULD YOU RATHER...

Go to a museum
or
a theme park?

Swim with dolphins
or
have meerkats climb all over you?

WOULD YOU RATHER...

Climb a mountain
or
go potholing?

Live in a castle in the Amazon jungle
or
a castle in the Sahara desert?

WOULD YOU RATHER...

Swim with dolphins
or
sharks?

Wake up in the middle of a forest
or
wake up in a rowing boat on a stretch
of water?

WOULD YOU RATHER...

Play paintball
or
do a laser tag?

Sail a yacht
or
go in the rapids in a dinghy?

WOULD YOU RATHER...

Eat a slice Brussel sprout flavored cakes

Or

Or a piece of meat-flavored chocolate?

Eat a chocolate-covered ant

Or

a spicy crispy locust?

WOULD YOU RATHER...

Go on a small sailing boat
or
a large ship?

Do your own stunts in a movie
or
have a stunt person do these for you?

WOULD YOU RATHER...

Have a magic carpet
or
a time travel machine?

Sail on the water in a ship
or
be below the water in a submarine?

WOULD YOU RATHER...

Attempt an escape room

or

a virtual reality game?

Go on an African safari trip

or

Stay in Igloo with the Eskimos?

WOULD YOU RATHER…

Spend time on a desert island alone
or
go on a large group holiday with
friends?

Snorkel in the Great Barrier Reef
or
go on an Airboat in the Everglades?

WOULD YOU RATHER...

Eat a raw potato
Or
an unsweetened grapefruit?

Eat healthy vegetables that taste like candy
Or
drink fruit juice instead of water for 1 year?

WOULD YOU RATHER...

Swim in the ocean
or
a pool?

Watch your favorite cartoon every morning
or
have ice-cream for breakfast every morning?

WOULD YOU RATHER...

Jump out of a plane with a parachute
Or
do a bungee jump?

See a firework display set to music
Or
watch a live band?

WOULD YOU RATHER...

Spend time reading and sunbathing
near the pool,
Or
go and see tourist attractions?

Return to a holiday destination you've
previously been to,
Or
explore somewhere new that may be
dangerous or boring?

WOULD YOU RATHER...

Eat a lasagna cupcake
or
a slice of cricket cake?

Eat a ham sandwich containing
chocolate
or
chocolate containing bits of ham?

WOULD YOU RATHER...

Visit a castle
or
visit an aquarium?

Stay in an Igloo and see the Northern
Lights for a week

or

stay in a tropical tree-top lodge by the
Amazon river for a week?

WOULD YOU RATHER...

Go diving in the Kingdom of Atlantis

or

Visit the International Space Station?

Drive a golf-buggy

or

go zip-lining?

WOULD YOU RATHER...

Have a go on a pogo-stick

or

play hide and seek?

Visit a huge secret garden
or
be locked in a toy shop at night?

WOULD YOU RATHER...

Take part in a pirate adventure
or
a space adventure?

Stop your country from being invaded
by an enemy army

or

prevent your country from
contracting a deadly disease?

WOULD YOU RATHER...

Eat fish and chips for dinner every night
or
a bacon cheeseburger every breakfast?

Drink a glass of spoiled milk
or
eat a rotten egg?

WOULD YOU RATHER...

See a volcano erupt

or

see the Grand Canyon?

Save the life of someone you've never met before

or

rescue two animals from a horrible fate?

WOULD YOU RATHER...

Slide down a long water slide

or

go in a jacuzzi?

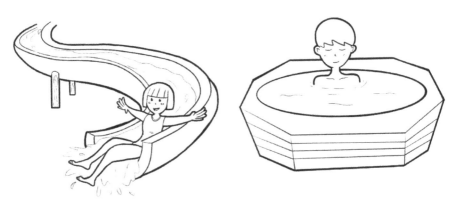

Make the discovery of a new animal on
a previously unexplored island

or

a new exotic plant?

WOULD YOU RATHER...

Feel too warm
or
feel too chilly?

Go on a roller-coaster
or
use a Virtual Reality headset?

WOULD YOU RATHER...

Be very intelligent

or

very funny?

Go sand surfing in the Sahara desert
or
surfing in Hawaii?

WOULD YOU RATHER...

Be the most well dressed in the world
or
the cleverest?

Have a very high IQ
or
be able to sing well in any style of your
choosing?

WOULD YOU RATHER...

Time travel to the past
or
into the future?

Make small differences in the lives of twenty individuals

or

a huge difference to the lives of two people?

WOULD YOU RATHER...

Be very lucky
or
very rich?

Have been born in the 1960s
or
2016?

WOULD YOU RATHER...

Choose wealth
or
health for the rest of your life?

 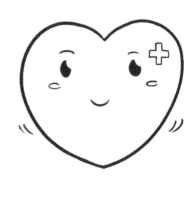

Be able to perfectly impersonate any
voice you hear
or
write in any language?

WOULD YOU RATHER...

Save each stray animal you meet
or
help out each homeless person?

Live indoors for 6 months or live
outdoor for months?

WOULD YOU RATHER...

Have three wishes granted
Or
be the richest person in the world?

Be able to recognize any piece of
music ever played by just a few notes
Or
be able to sing with perfect pitch?

WOULD YOU RATHER...

Live without electricity
or
live without fresh water?

Be without food
or
a safe place to sleep?

WOULD YOU RATHER...

Eat a healthy diet
Or
exercise regularly?

Be a genius in a world of foolish
people

or

a fool in a world of geniuses?

WOULD YOU RATHER...

Be completely alone for 5 years
or
never alone for more than 5 minutes?

Save the life of an elderly relative
or
save the life of a child who is not
related to you?

WOULD YOU RATHER...

Live without the Internet

or

live without being able to control your surrounding temperature (hot and cold)?

Live a hundred years in the future

or

a hundred years in the past?

WOULD YOU RATHER...

Have magical powers

or

superpowers?

Be wealthy in a job you dislike
or
poor in a job you love?

WOULD YOU RATHER...

Never age

Or

never need to sleep?

Be able to eat anything without
putting on weight
Or
never need to eat at all?

Did you enjoy the book?

If you did, we are ecstatic. If not, please write your complaint to us and we will make sure to fix it.

If you're feeling generous, there is something important that you can help me with – tell other people that you enjoyed the book.

Ask a grown-up to write about it on Amazon. When they do, more people will find out about the book. It also lets Amazon know that we are making kids around the world laugh. Even a few words and ratings would go a long way.

If you have any ideas or jokes that you think are super funny, please let us know. We would love to hear from you. Our email address is - riddleland@riddlelandforkids.com

Alert: Riddleland Bonus

Join our special Facebook Joke Group at

~Riddleland For Kids~

or

send an email to:

Riddleland@riddlelandforkids.com

and you will get the following

- 50 Bonus Jokes and Riddles
- An Entry in Our Monthly Giveaway of $50 Amazon Gift card!
- Early Access to new books

We draw a new winner each month and will contact you via email or the Facebook group.

Good Luck!

Would you like your jokes and riddles to be featured in our next book?

We are having a contest to see who are the smartest or funniest boys and girls in the world!

1) **Creative and Challenging Riddles**

2) **Tickle Your Funny Bone Contest**

Parents, please email us your child's "Original" Riddle or Joke, **and he or she could win a new Riddleland book and be featured in our next book.**

Here are the rules:

1) It must be challenging for the riddles and funny for the jokes!

2) It must be 100% Original and not something from the Internet! It is easy to find out!

3) You can submit both a joke and a riddle as they are 2 separate contests.

4) No help from the parents unless they are as funny as you.

5) Winners will be announced via email or our Facebook group – Riddleland for kids

6) Please also mention what book you purchased.

7) Email us at Riddleland@riddlelandforkids.com

Other Fun Children's Books for Kids!

Riddles Series

Try Not to Laugh Challenge Series

Would You Rather... Series

Get them on Amazon

or our website at www.riddlelandforkids.com

About Riddleland

Riddleland is a mum + dad run publishing company. We are passionate about creating fun and innovative books to help children develop their reading skills and fall in love with reading. If you have suggestions for us or want to work with us, shoot us an email at riddleland@riddlelandforkids.com

Our family's favorite quote

"Creativity is an area in which younger people have a tremendous advantage since they have an endearing habit of always questioning past wisdom and authority." - Bill Hewlett